Monarch Butterfly

by

Harry Goldcroft

PIB Publishing
13 Pencross View
Hemyock
Cullompton
Devon. EX15 3XH
United Kingdom

DISCLAIMER

This book is intended for information and educational purposes only. While every attempt has been made to verify the facts and information provided herein, neither the author nor publisher assumes any responsibility for errors, inaccuracies or omissions, and specifically disclaim any implied warranties or merchantability or fitness for any particular purpose and shall in no event be liable for any loss of profit or any other commercial damage, including but not limited to special, incidental, consequential, or other damages.

In addition, neither the author nor publisher makes any guarantees, including but not limited to any express or implied endorsement of any the organizations, sites or other references listed in this book as resources for further information, assistance, equipment, or other uses. And the reader expressly assumes all risk in dealing with these sources . Furthermore, while accurate at the time of original publication, due to the ever changing nature of the internet and the world we live in addresses, links, urls, phones numbers and/or individual contact persons may not have changed.

Any slights of people or organizations are unintentional.

This book was printed in the UK and USA.

Dedication

To the many organisations and trusts around the world that dedicate their time and share their passion for butterflies.

In particular the Monarch Butterfly that is an amazing creature. It can travel thousands of miles when migrating and sadly are struggling in their environment with numbers coming down all the time.

There are several links in my book where further information can be obtained.

Table of Contents

Chapter 1. Introduction

I don't remember the first time I saw a Monarch Butterfly but I do remember the first time I saw a large gathering of them. It was a relatively cool day in late summer and as I was walking my dog, a tree ahead of me shimmered in the sunlight.

From a distance, it looked as though a breeze was blowing through the leaves, causing a nervous dance of movement. I didn't think much of it; simply kept walking. As I drew a few feet from the tree, the movement captured my attention once more and I focused clearly on what I was seeing.

It wasn't the leaves that were dancing in the wind but butterflies, hundreds of Monarch Butterflies to be precise, that were fluttering their wings. Occasionally, one would lift up and drift through the air before coming to rest again on the tree.

It was breathtaking, the flashes of orange and the contrasting darker colors. I was captivated and spent hours watching the butterflies. For days, they gathered there, the number growing, until they finally dispersed and continued on their migration; every day I would watch them and it was almost heartbreaking when they finally disappeared from sight.

But while they were gone, they had left behind an interest in butterflies that I have maintained for years. Studying and watching Monarch Butterflies is a hobby that people everywhere enjoy. In fact, many people travel to see these amazing insects during their migration and over the winter months. They are beautiful creatures that inspire the masses.

And that is what this book is all about, inspiring the masses and giving them the tools they need to understand these beautiful insects. In this book, I go over the traits of a Monarch Butterfly, what they eat through all the life stages and also what those life stages are.

In addition to the fascinating facts about the Monarch Butterfly, I will take you through ways that you can make your garden a friendly place for the butterfly. Finally, for those enthusiasts that want to try, this book will also take you through raising your own Monarch Butterflies to release.

So sit back and enjoy this comprehensive guide on the Monarch Butterfly.

Chapter 2. Getting to know the Monarch Butterfly

Let me introduce you to the world of butterflies, or more specifically, to the world of monarch butterflies. For the most part, everyone knows what a monarch butterfly is but before we look at raising monarch's or what is affecting their habitat, I want to take the time to properly introduce you to the monarch butterfly.

This chapter will go over what a monarch butterfly is, what they eat and the general facts about the monarch butterfly. Once we know all the general facts, we can move forward and learn even more about this breathtaking insect.

1. What is the Monarch Butterfly?

The monarch butterfly, which is also known as the Danaus plexippus, is a beautiful orange butterfly with contrasting black webbing on the wings and white dots. It is one of the most well known species of butterflies alive today.

The monarch butterfly is what is also known as a milkweed butterfly. The reason for this is because monarch butterflies lay their eggs on poisonous milkweed plants and the larvae, also known as a caterpillar, eat the leaves of the milkweed. The monarch butterflies diet when it is in the larval stage makes it a poisonous butterfly to many predators.

While we often think of monarch butterflies as a smaller butterfly, they are actually quite large and can have a wingspan up to 12.4cm or 4.88 inches. They are primarily found in North America and they are known for having one of the longest migration patterns on earth. Every year, hundreds of thousands of monarch butterflies make the trip from their overwintering home in Mexico and Southern California to Canada and then back again.

However, while the monarch butterfly is primarily thought of as a North American Butterfly, it has been seen around the world. In fact, in 1871, the monarch butterfly was found in both New Zealand and Australia. In Australia, it is known as the wanderer.

Other places that it has been found are the United Kingdom, Western Europe, the Canary Islands and Madeira. It is important to note that while some of the European monarch butterflies will migrate small distances, it is the North American monarch butterfly that has the longest migration pattern.

2. What do Monarch Butterflies Eat?

While I go over the types of food that you can plant in a garden for your monarch butterfly friendly yard later on in this book, I want to take the time to go

over the things that a monarch butterfly will eat as a general fact about them.

When we are looking at the food that a monarch butterfly eats, we need to actually look at both the larval stage and the adult stage. If you are not aware of it, adult monarch butterflies have a different diet than a caterpillar.

a) Caterpillar Food

Monarch butterfly caterpillars are actually a caterpillar that only eats a single food and that is milkweed. While it may seem limited, there are over 2000 species of milkweed around the world and the monarch caterpillar will eat all of them.

If there is no milkweed when the female is ready to lay her eggs, she will either not lay them or she will choose the wrong plant. If she chooses the wrong plant, the caterpillars will die.

There are no other foods that the caterpillar will eat and it is the milkweed juice that makes them poisonous to other animals.

b) Adult Butterfly Food

Unlike the caterpillar, the monarch butterfly can eat a range of different nectars from plants. It should be noted that adult monarch butterflies only eat nectar and no longer eat the leaves of a milkweed plant.

They will eat the nectar of flowers by using their long straw like mouth known as a proboscis. The proboscis is curled up when they are not feeding. When they are feeding, they will uncurl the proboscis and sip at the nectar.

In addition to nectar, monarch butterflies will also drink water and will sip at sodium in soil for minerals and nutrients. This is more commonly seen in male monarch butterflies; however, females will also do this.

While they will feed from a wide range of flowers, the monarch butterfly does require access to fall wildflowers since these flowers will provide them with the proper nutrients for their migration south.

That being said, there are many flowers that the monarch butterfly will feed from, including the following:

Plant #1: Garden Phlox

This pretty little plant is known for its clusters of pink flowers that bloom in late summer, early fall. It is a plant that attracts many types of butterflies including the monarch butterfly; however, it is not the preferred food of the monarch.

Plant #2: Goldenrod

Although it is seen as a weed, goldenrod is one of the preferred foods of the monarch butterfly. While many people have mistaken goldenrod as a plant that affects allergy sufferers, it actually doesn't and is simply a beautiful plant that blooms through summer and autumn. The plant should have yellow blossoms.

Plant #3: Butterfly Milkweed

This plant is something that both the adult monarch butterfly and the caterpillar will enjoy as it provides a food source for both. The bright, orange flowers will provide nectar for monarchs while the green leaves is the perfect place to lay eggs and feed caterpillars.

Plant #4: Blanket Flower

These bright orange and yellow flowers are a beautiful plant to have in a garden and they attract many types of butterflies, including monarchs. The plant is actually very easy to care for and will do well with very little help from a gardener.

Plant #5: Black-Eyed Susan

This pretty yellow plant with the dark brown to black center is a popular plant for butterflies and for butterfly gardeners. It is a plant that blooms well into the fall and monarchs are drawn to it as a main food source.

Plant #6: Blazing Star

This purple flower can add a lot of color to any garden and it is a flower that will draw bees and butterflies to your yard. The flower resembles a spike of flowers with grass like leaves on the plant.

Plant #7: Bee Balm

Just as it sounds, this is a plant that attracts honey bees and is also perfect for attracting butterflies. The plant has a tall stem with clusters of flowers on top; however the flowers can be red, purple or pink.

Plant #8: New England Aster

New England Aster is a flower that I strongly recommend when you are making a butterfly garden since monarch butterflies love this purple flower with its abundant petals.

Plant #9: Joe Pye Weed

Another plant that monarch butterflies love, this purple plant with long stalks of over 6 feet will attract butterflies, bees and even hummingbirds. While it is not a staple plant for monarch butterflies, it is a plant that will attract them.

Plant #10: Purple Coneflower

Coneflowers are quite beautiful with their large drooping petals and purple coloring. In addition, they are very easy to grow and require very little work. The added bonus is that monarch butterflies love them and will often stop to take a sip of nectar when they see them.

And there are the plants that you will see a monarch butterfly adult drinking from. I have also included a few other plants that you can grow in the section on maintaining a butterfly friendly yard.

3. Facts about the Monarch Butterfly

Now that we know what monarch butterflies and their caterpillars eat, let's learn some of the general facts about the butterfly. You may be surprised how many interesting facts there are about this beautiful insect.

Q: Can monarch butterflies live in any climate?

A: While the monarch butterfly has been found throughout the world, they need warmer weather to survive. That is actually one of the reasons why monarch butterflies migrate such long distances.

Monarchs need the warmth of the sun over winter, which is why they migrate to their overwintering sites in Mexico and Southern California and they need the milkweed that is found in Canada to lay their eggs.

Q: Why do they need warmth?

A: Monarch butterflies are cold blooded and cannot survive cold temperatures. To ensure the success of future generations, the monarch butterflies will fly south to avoid the cold weather.

Q: Are there different patterns of color in Monarch Butterflies?

A: While monarch butterflies all have white, orange and black on their wings, there are many different patterns that you will see in a monarch. The webbing in each monarch butterfly can be slightly different and there are main differences in the webbing between male and female.

Q: How long does it take for an egg to hatch?

A: This varies depending on the egg, the time of year and what generation of butterfly it is but usually, the egg hatches within 4 to 5 days after being laid.

Q: Do monarch butterflies lay eggs on any plant?

A: No, monarch butterflies will only lay eggs on milkweed; however, when there is no milkweed available, the female may lay them on other plants. When this happens, the caterpillars will not survive as they need milkweed.

Q: How many eggs do monarch butterflies lay?

A: Unlike many other butterflies, monarch butterflies do not lay a large number of eggs at once. Instead, they only lay one egg at a time on a single leaf.

While they only lay one egg at a time, it does not mean that the monarch butterfly does not lay a lot of eggs. They can lay anywhere from 500 to 700 eggs over their lifetime and they will lay several dozen in one day. In fact, they can lay up to 200 eggs in one day.

Q: Do monarch butterflies need both male and female butterflies to produce eggs?

A: Yes, to produce fertilized eggs, the male and female butterfly must mate. If the female does not mate, she will not produce fertilized eggs. Fertilization occurs inside the female butterfly and not outside.

Q: Do monarch butterflies die after they lay their eggs?

A: No, female monarch butterflies do not die after they lay their eggs. They can actually live for several weeks after laying and will die of old age, or predation, and not from laying eggs.

Q: How long does a caterpillar stay a caterpillar?

A: The lifespan of the caterpillar stage differs again due to the abundance of food, time of year and so on but the monarch caterpillar is usually in the larval stage for about 2 weeks.

Q: Do they spin their chrysalis?

A: .The monarch caterpillar will spin a small amount of silk onto the leaf or plant that they are hanging from but it is only a small button, not an actual cocoon.

It is actually a misconception that the pupa or chrysalis is spun. Instead, it is actually under the skin when they shed their final skin. The chrysalis is soft and fleshy at first but within an hour, it is hard and protective.

Q: How long do they stay in their chrysalis?

A: A monarch caterpillar stays in its pupa, or chrysalis, for about 9 to 14 days. The average is roughly 10 days before the monarch butterfly emerges.

Q: Can you help a monarch butterfly get out of its pupa?

A: No, you should always allow a monarch butterfly, or any butterfly for that matter, to get out of their pupa on their own. The struggles of the monarch help reduce the size of the abdomen and help dry the crumpled and wet wings.

Q: After becoming an adult butterfly, how long does a monarch butterfly live?

A: The lifespan of monarch butterflies vary depending on the time of year that they are born. Most live 2 to 6 weeks after their metamorphosis, while others can live up to one or two years. The reason for this is because monarch's born right before fall become the monarchs that migrate. They will be the ones that fly to the overwintering site and head north again in the early spring.

Q: Will a monarch butterfly lay eggs on plants other than milkweed?

A: A female will try to hold onto her eggs for as long as she can to prevent laying on anything but milkweed. However, occasionally it does happen but any caterpillars hatched on plants other than milkweed will die.

Q: Can you raise monarch butterflies?

A: Yes, you can raise them quite easily and I have covered that later on in this book.

Q: Can you tell the difference between a male and female monarch butterfly?

A: As adults, yes, there are distinct markings that are seen only on males. Read the chapter on anatomy to learn more.

During the larval stage, however, there is no way that you can tell unless you dissect the caterpillar to look for male reproductive organs.

Q: Can cold temperatures, when the butterfly is in the pupa stage, affect the growth of wings?

A: Yes, cold weather can affect the development of a pupa and the result can be deformed wings. It can also result in the death of the monarch butterfly if the temperatures drop too low.

Q: Is there a difference between a chrysalis and a chyrsalid?

A: Both terms are heard frequently and the answer is that no, there is no difference. Both refer to the pupa stage of the monarch's lifecycle.

Q: Why do monarch butterflies migrate?

A: The reason why monarch butterflies migrate is because they are cold blooded and need the warmth to survive. For this reason, when the days become cooler, the monarch butterflies will shut down their reproduction system, hibernate in a sense, and will begin to migrate south.

During the spring of the following year, the days will start to lengthen, which will signal to the monarchs that it is time to breed and begin their migration north.

The reason why they migrate north is to find the important milkweed that their larvae need to survive.

Q: Are monarch butterflies at risk?

A: Yes, monarch butterflies are at risk and they are continually at risk every year. Environmental factors, human encroachment, disease and predation affect monarch butterflies yearly and only a small number of eggs hatch and reach maturity.

Q: Is there a way I can help?

A: Yes, there are many ways that you can help monarch populations from planting a monarch butterfly friendly yard to raising your own population of butterflies.

And you can help by reading the rest of this book so let's get started and move forward.

Chapter 3. Anatomy of the Monarch Butterfly

Before we get into the lifecycle of the monarch butterfly, I feel that it is important to truly understand the anatomy of the monarch butterfly. This chapter will go over everything that you need to know about their anatomy and I will also cover the adult monarch, the egg, the pupa and the caterpillar as each stage creates different sections of anatomy.

One thing that I should mention before we move on to the anatomy is that monarch butterflies are cold blooded creatures. What this means is that they are not capable of regulating their own body temperature. They rely on the sun to warm them and this one of the reasons why they cannot hibernate in northern climates through the winter months.

As with the adults, the caterpillars also need warmer climates to survive and they are designed to thrive on milkweed. Without milkweed, the caterpillars will succumb to starvation.

Now that I have gone over those two important points on anatomy, let's look at the anatomy of each stage of life for the monarch butterfly.

1. Anatomy of the Egg

The anatomy of the monarch butterfly egg is actually very basic and there isn't a lot that we need to cover in this. Monarch butterflies lay small eggs that are not much larger than a pinhead.

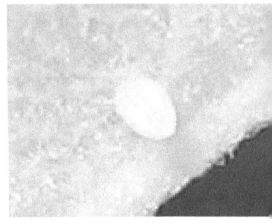

The eggs are white in coloration but as the day for hatching draws near, they will change to a pale color. The anatomy of the egg is very simple. They are an oval shaped egg with the largest width of the egg being the section that holds onto the leaf.

The egg is actually quite hard for an insect egg and is covered with a hard shell called the chorion. This helps protect the young inside the egg from both predators and the elements.

Inside the shell, there is a layer of wax that will keep the egg moist so the caterpillar can grow safely. Although it is very hard to see it with the naked eye, under a microscope, the egg actually has many funnel shaped openings at one end. These openings are called micropyles and are actually used for fertilization. When the male butterfly breeds with the female, the sperm go into the funnel-shaped openings to fertilize the egg.

In addition to these openings, there should be tiny ridges running down the monarch butterfly egg. These should start at the slightly pointed end and run the length of the egg. Although it is not clear why there are ridges on the egg, we do know that they are formed in the female before she lays the egg.

And that is all there is to know about the anatomy of the egg. The caterpillar does chew its way out of the end that is not attached to the leaf and never at the sides or bottom.

2. Anatomy of the Caterpillar

While the egg is quite basic when it comes to anatomy, the caterpillar itself is not. In fact, a caterpillar is a complex insect that is designed for a specific job. This is a creature that can eat through a milkweed leaf in less than an hour and still be ready to eat more.

When we look at the anatomy of the caterpillar, we are actually looking at three parts of the caterpillar. If you are not aware, caterpillars have three distinct body parts. These are the abdomen, thorax and the head.

To start, the head is usually larger than the body of the caterpillar when it first hatches. In general, it doesn't change much in shape and size from when it is first hatched.

The head should have two antennae that are actually near the bottom of the head instead of at the top. The antennae are very short compared to the adult monarch butterfly. In addition, there should be an upper and lower lip as well as a pair of mandibles that are used for chewing.

Under the mouth there is a maxillary palp, which is a small bump under the mouth on either side of the spinneret, which the caterpillar uses to create a silk thread. The maxillary palp and antennae are used to help locate and direct food to the caterpillar.

The upper half of the caterpillar's head has two head capculs that look very similar to eyes; however, they are not eyes. In actuality, the monarch caterpillar has very poor eyesight and it has six pairs of eyes. These eyes are very simple and are called ocelli.

Finally, the head of the caterpillar should have two filaments on it, which are often confused with antennae as they are long and thick. However, while they do serve as a sensory organ, the primary sensory organs are the maxillary palps and antennae.

The first part of the caterpillar, after the head, is known as the thorax. On the thorax is a pair of jointed legs. There are actually three segments to the thorax, which are known as the thoracic segment. Each segment has a pair of true legs, which the caterpillar uses to grip onto the plant and to move around.

After the thorax is the abdomen. Like the thorax, the abdomen is segmented and there are roughly 10 segments. Each segment located between the third and sixth segment, should have a pair of prolegs, which are fake legs. While they are not considered to be the true legs of a monarch caterpillar, they do have a tiny hook in them that attaches to the leaf, securing the caterpillar to the plant.

Along the abdomen and the thorax, there should be small holes on the monarch caterpillar. These holes are called spiracles and they are actually connected to tracheae, which are long tubes used to carry oxygen to the body of the caterpillar.

Finally, on the back end of the monarch caterpillar, there should be a pair of filaments that are also used as a sensory organ.

When it comes to coloration, the monarch caterpillar should have bands of black, yellow and white. There should also be white spots on the prolegs. One thing that is interesting to note is that the colors are actually there to aid the caterpillar.

Believe it or not, the colors of the caterpillar are used for temperature regulation. The black absorbs the heat of the sun, which allows the caterpillar to warm up on cold days. The yellow and white reflect sunlight so they help the caterpillar stay cooler.

In addition, while the majority of caterpillars have a ratio of coloring being 50% black and 25% of each yellow and white, there are slight changes to the coloration depending on where the caterpillar lives. If they live in cooler climates, the caterpillar will have blacker and thicker bands. If the caterpillar lives in warmer climates, there is less black and more yellow and white.

There is a genetic abnormality that can occur in monarch caterpillars and this is when the monarch caterpillar lacks the yellow bands and is only black and white. These caterpillars are known as Zebras and it is still unclear why the mutation occurs. The only thing we know is that the butterfly of the zebra caterpillar is no different from any other monarch butterfly.

To close on this section, it is important to note that coloration is also a defensive trait since the bright colors of the monarch caterpillar lets predators, such as birds, know that these caterpillars are unsavory.

3. Anatomy of the Pupa

Like the egg, the anatomy of the pupa is quite simple and does not need a lot of explanation. One thing that most people don't realize is that the pupa, which is also known as a chrysalis is under the final skin of the caterpillar.

When the caterpillar sheds its final skin, or exoskeleton, the pupa is under that and is not something that the caterpillar creates.

With that in mind, there are actually several sections to the pupa. The first is a silk button that attaches to the plant the caterpillar is hanging from.

Attached to that button is a cremaster, which is found at the hind end of the caterpillar. This is a small hook that attaches to the button and keeps the pupa secured to the plant.

Under the cremaster is where the rest of the caterpillar is with the abdomen being directly under the cremaster.

The wings, or where the wings are developed are in the middle section of the pupa and the head of the insect is in the very bottom.

When the pupa is first formed, it is very soft to the touch; however, after about an hour, the pupa hardens and will protect the caterpillar through the metamorphosis.

The color of the chrysalis is actually clear, however, there is a green coloration to it since you are seeing the pupa inside. As the metamorphosis goes on, the color inside the chrysalis changes and you will be able to see the butterfly before it emerges.

4. Anatomy of the Monarch Butterfly

Now that we have gone through all the other parts of the life cycle, it is time to look at the actual anatomy of the monarch butterfly. Before we do, it is interesting to note that while the monarch butterfly looks completely different from its caterpillar, there are several areas of the monarch butterfly that is similar.

When we look at a butterfly, we generally break it down into four sections. These are the head, thorax, wings and abdomen.

The head of the monarch butterfly has the eyes, palpi, proboscis and the antennae and it looks slightly different from the caterpillar head.

While the caterpillar had very simple eyesight, this is not the case with the adult monarch butterfly. In fact, the monarch butterfly has very complex eyes and it consists of two large compounds that are made up of thousands of ommatidia, which are optical panels or units in the butterfly's eye. In fact, there can be up to 17000 ommatidia in the eyes. These ommatidia sense both light and images and give the monarch butterfly exceptional eyesight.

In addition to the eyes, the monarch butterflies have two antennae that emerge from between the eyes. These antennae are segmented and can be held at various angles. It is not clear why butterflies move their antennae around but it is believed to be used as a form of radar. It is also believed that the antennae are used to pick up pheromones and to determine the nutrients in soil.

In fact, many have seen monarch butterflies engage in "dipping", which is when the butterfly will place its antennal tips onto soil. This enables the butterfly to determine if there is sodium in the moisture, which males need for copulation.

The antennae of the monarch butterfly are covered in scales, hairs and olfactory pits. There are actually over 160000 olfactory sensors that the butterfly uses to pick up scents in the air.

In addition to the antennae, butterflies also have two palpi, which are two protrusions on the head. They are small and they are also covered in the olfactory sensors. It is unclear what the palpi are there for but it is believed that it is actually sensitive to food sources for the adult butterfly.

The final item on the head that we should address is the proboscis. This is actually the butterfly's tongue and is a straw like structure that sucks the nectar from the flowers.

Although it may seem quite simple, the proboscis is actually two interlocking c-section channels. Together they create the drinking straw tube that is often coiled up when the butterfly is not drinking. Inside the proboscis are actually olfactory sensors that enable the butterfly to taste what it is eating. In addition, the two c-section channels can be broken apart by the butterfly so it can clean any sticky fluids that may have clogged the tube.

Under the head of the butterfly is the thorax, the same as when you look at a caterpillar. There are three segments and on each segment, there is a pair of legs.

Each of the legs is made up of six segments, which help the butterfly stabilize itself on items. Each leg has a tarsus, which is also known as tarsi in plural, on the bottom. The tarsi work as feet and will grip things the butterfly lands on. On each of the tarsus is a organ that allows the butterfly to taste things that they are landing on.

One thing that should be mentioned is that the monarch butterfly often looks like it only has four legs. The reason for this is that the front legs are usually curled up against the thorax.

On the thorax, the four wings of the monarch butterfly can be found. Wings come off of the butterfly on the second and third thorax segment. The monarch has two hindwings and two forewings and they are attached to the thorax by muscles so the wings can be moved as the butterfly changes the shape of its thorax.

The wings themselves are quite delicate and are filled with veins and nerves. Actually, it is the veins in the wing that give the strength, support and structure to the wings. The veins also help cool the butterfly off when it is too hot.

The membrane that is covering the wing of the monarch butterfly is transparent but they are covered with tiny scales that create the color of the wing.

The scales are extremely small and there are actually 600 individual scales per square millimetre of wing surface. The more scales there are per square millimeter, the darker and more vibrant the coloring.

When we look at the scales, we are actually looking at three different types of scales. These are

- ***Pigmentary Scales:*** These scales are flat and have several chemical pigments in them. Most of the pigments are due to larval food plant that the monarch caterpillar eats. Pigment scales account for black, red and orange, however, it is how the scales cover the wing that lead to the cream and orange colors that are seen in the species. In addition to the pigments, subtle variations to the pigmentation of each scale will create texture and shading.

  The scales are also known as ground scales as they are the primary scale that gives the color and pattern. It is important to note that the pigment scales are laid out in neat rows and each row is actually alternating rows of pigmentary and structural scales.

- ***Structural Scales:*** Structural scales are larger scales that overlap pigment scales. They are actually semi transparent and this allows for light to pass through the scale and be refracted or diffracted to produce a pattern of light. When we see the structural scales, it is usually when we see a vibrant color such as fluorescent orange or metallic gold on the wing. However, many of the colors that the structural scales create is not visible to humans and can only be detected by other butterflies.

- ***Androconia Scales:*** Although these can be found on all butterflies, they are mainly found on male butterflies. They actually appear as streaks or patches of dark coloration on the forewings. At the base of each scale is a tiny sac that is filled with pheromones and it is these sacs that help males attract females.

Now that we have covered the wings of the monarch butterfly, it is time to look at the final area of anatomy and that is the abdomen. Like the caterpillar, there are several segments in the thorax. In actuality, there are eleven segments on the monarch butterfly abdomen but the last three segments are joined together.

As with the caterpillar, there should be small holes on the monarch butterfly. These holes are called spiracles and they are actually connected to tracheae, which are long tubes used to carry oxygen to the body of the monarch butterfly.

The adult butterfly is a striking butterfly with deep orange wings that are outlined in black. White dots also cover the body and edges of the wings.

As you can see, the anatomy of the monarch butterfly is quite complex and it is important to understand all the different aspects of the anatomy so you can understand the insect itself.

Chapter 4. Lifecycle of the Monarch Butterfly

As you know, most people know the lifecycle of a butterfly and the lifecycle of a monarch butterfly is not that different. While most people are aware of the lifecycle of butterflies, it is still important to go over it in this book to help you understand monarch butterflies.

Before we begin, I want to stress that monarch butterflies go through several stages in their lifetime. In fact, they go through four stages, which I will go through in this chapter.

In addition to the stages, monarch butterflies also have generations. A generation is all of the butterflies born at the same time in the same population. Those butterflies go through the four stages until they finally lay eggs as an adult. After that point, the next generation is born and the older generations begin to die off.

Although we know from the prior chapter that monarch butterflies can live for several years, most monarch butterflies only have an adult lifespan of a few months. Instead, there is are new generations being born throughout the year and monarch butterflies actually have four generations in one year.

The reason why I am explaining this is because it can be quite confusing and there is a common misconception that the same monarch butterflies migrate year after year. This is not the case and I will explain it further in this chapter but for now, let's look at the stages of the monarch butterflies lifecycle.

1. Stage One: The Egg

Also known as an ovum, the monarch butterfly is a species of butterfly that only lays one egg at a time. In fact, the egg of the monarch butterfly is laid under the leaf of a milkweed plant. They generally

choose a healthy leaf to lay the egg.

While the monarch butterfly only lays one egg at a time, a female butterfly can lay up to 500 eggs in her lifespan. In addition, the female and male butterfly breed before she lays the eggs so the eggs are fertilized when she lays them.

The egg of the monarch butterfly is very small, about the size of a pinhead measuring 1.2mm by 0.9mm and weighing only 0.46mg, and they are oval in shape. The egg should have tiny lines that run from the top to the bottom of the egg. They are creamy-white in coloration, however, they do change to a pale yellow closer to hatching.

Once the egg is laid, it actually only takes four days for the caterpillar to hatch out of the egg. It is important that if you find a caterpillar egg to simply leave it where it is. You can mark the location and check it frequently to watch the caterpillar hatch out.

2. Stage Two: The Caterpillar

At around day four, the caterpillar begins to chew its way out of the egg. After it has emerged from the egg, the caterpillar will start to consume the eggshell that it just hatched out of. This is actually a very important step for the caterpillar since they receive many vitamins and minerals from that egg shell that will aid in development.

When we look at caterpillars, we are actually looking at several stages, which are known as instars. To be specific, an instar is a period between molts, which is when the caterpillar sheds its old skin.

Every butterfly species has a number of instars with their larva and it differs from species to species. The monarch butterfly caterpillar has five instars and I will go through each stage of the caterpillar so you can understand how the caterpillar develops.

a) First Instar

The very first instar of a monarch caterpillar's life starts from the moment the caterpillar emerges from its shell. It should only be about 2 to 3 millimeters long.

The coloring of the monarch caterpillar at this stage is not as vibrant as you will see later. In fact, they tend to be a grayish caterpillar with bands of black on them.

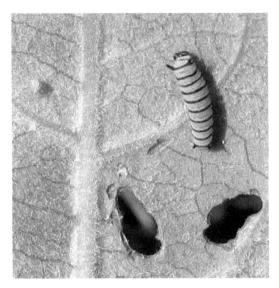

As I mentioned, when the caterpillar enters the first instar, it will eat its own eggshell. Once the eggshell is consumed, the caterpillar will begin to eat the milkweed leaf that it was born on.

One interesting fact about this first meal is that it can be fatal to the caterpillar. In fact, many caterpillars die after eating the milkweed leaf. The main reason for this is that the milkweed leaf excretes a latex that acts like glue. Many caterpillars die after eating the lip because their mouths get closed shut due to the milkweed gum covering it.

For the caterpillars that survive the first meal, the consumption of their leaf marks the end of the first instar. At this time, the caterpillar will become very still and will begin to shed its skin. Do not disturb the caterpillar if you find one that is being very still as you can disrupt the molting process.

b) Second Instar

After that first molting process, the second instar begins for the caterpillar. At this time, you should begin to see the vibrant coloration of the monarch caterpillar. It should be a striking caterpillar of yellow black and white. The colors should band the caterpillar and should appear as stripes on the caterpillar. The head should be striped with yellow and black with two black filaments, which are long thin appendages that are found on caterpillars on the head. In addition, there should be two black filaments on the back end of the caterpillar as well.

During this stage, the caterpillar is about a ¼ inch in length or 6 and a half millimeters. They spend much of their day eating milkweed leaves. Generally, this instar lasts until the caterpillar has eaten one or two more leaves.

As with the first instar, the end of this instar occurs when the caterpillar sheds its skin. Again, the caterpillar will become very still when it is about to shed its skin so do not disturb it if you find a still caterpillar.

c) Third Instar

The third instar is very similar to the second instar. The caterpillar continues to eat milkweed leaves and continues to grow in size. At this stage, the caterpillar should be about 15 to 16 millimetres in size so it is almost an inch at this point.

In addition to a greater size, the caterpillar is looking different in coloration. It will still have the same black, yellow and white bands but the coloring is becoming more vibrant.

In addition, the three sets of legs will be more apparent and the front legs of the caterpillar will be closer to the head then they were originally. Finally, the filaments of the caterpillar will be longer and more noticeable.

When the caterpillar has reached the end of the third instar, he will shed his skin, or molt, again.

d) Fourth Instar

After the third instar, the caterpillar is really starting to come along in its development. At this stage, you should notice that the prolegs, which are a set of fake legs on the back half of the caterpillar, are well developed and evident.

You will also notice that these five sets of prolegs will have noticeable dogs of white on them.

In addition to the prolegs, the filaments on the head and back end of the caterpillar are also quite evident and are thick and black. The caterpillar should be about 1 inch in length.

Finally, the caterpillar will have a huge appetite during this instar and can easily eat through a single leaf in under an hour. They have a voracious appetite and will continue eating until they are ready to molt.

As will all of the instars to this point, the caterpillar will become still just before he sheds his skin. The instar ends with the molting process.

e) Fifth Instar

The final instar that you will see in the caterpillar stage is the fifth instar. During this time, the caterpillar should be at its full length of about 2 inches in length.

It should also be very plump as this is the final instar in the caterpillar's life. The prolegs should be well formed and the white dots on the prolegs should stand out. The coloration should be vibrant and the black bands on the monarch caterpillar should have a soft, velvety feel to them.

During this stage, the caterpillar will begin to break the petiole, which is the section, or stalk, that connects the leaf to the plant, when it is eating. Often, that is the best way to find a caterpillar by looking for a broken petiole on a plant.

While it may not have been a quick insect at its earlier stage, at this large stage, it is actually quite fast. This is because it is looking for the perfect spot to form its pupa.

When the caterpillar reaches the end of the fifth instar, and has found its resting spot, it will hang upside down from the leaf or plant. Once it is hanging from a small silk button, which is has spun; it will begin to shed its skin for the final time. After the skin has been shed, it will hang in a J like fashion and will become a pupa.

3. Stage Three: The Pupa

The pupa stage is one that most people are aware of since it is the stage when the metamorphosis, where the caterpillar becomes a butterfly. It generally takes two weeks for the caterpillar to change into a butterfly and during those two weeks, a lot is happening inside the pupa, which is also known as a chrysalis.

As I mentioned, the caterpillar will shed its skin for the final time in the fifth instar. However, one common misconception that people have is that the caterpillar will create the chrysalis when it is ready to begin the metamorphosis.

That is not the case and the casing for the chrysalis is actually under the caterpillar's skin when it molts the final time. The chrysalis is a jade green casing that will protect the caterpillar during the transformation.

When the skin is first shed, the chrysalis is soft and you should be able to see the shape of the caterpillar. After about an hour, the chrysalis will become a hard shell, which is smooth in appearance, that protects the caterpillar through the metamorphosis.

During the days after the pupa hardens, the caterpillar will go through several changes. For instance, the wings will begin to develop, the mouth of the caterpillar will change from one used for chewing to one that is used for sipping nectar. In addition, the legs of the caterpillar will change as well.

As the metamorphosis continues, the color of the pupa will change until it becomes a dark brown, or black. In addition, near the end of the metamorphosis, you should be able to see the orange and black wings of the monarch butterfly inside.

This stage ends when the adult butterfly emerges from the chrysalis. Although I did say two weeks, the actual time of metamorphosis differs between butterflies and can range from 9 to 14 days.

4. Stage Four: The Adult

Also known as a butterfly, the adult butterfly emerges from its chrysalis when it is fully developed. It is interesting to note that there is no set signal that lets people know a butterfly is about to emerge. There may be some movement to the pupa but this can be seen throughout the metamorphosis. Instead, the chrysalis will suddenly crack and the adult monarch butterfly will emerge.

It is very important that you do not interfere when the butterfly is emerging. This is a process that should be done over a course of time as the struggles of emerging from the chrysalis will aid in proper development. Without this struggle, a butterfly will, and often does, die.

As it is emerging, the body, or thorax, of the monarch butterfly is very large and swollen. In addition, the wings of the butterfly are small. The wings are actually crumpled and wet and as the butterfly struggles free and then begins to work its wings, the wings dry until they are the proper size and shape.

While this is occurring, the butterfly clings to the shell of its chrysalis and is vulnerable to predators during this stage. One thing that should be mentioned is that while the wings are drying, hemolymph, which is a blood like substance, begins pumping through the butterfly's body, which aids in the enlargement of the wings.

Once the wings are enlarged and dry, usually within an hour of emerging, the butterfly can begin its new life as an adult. This usually ranges in duration between 2 to 6 weeks; however, some generations of butterflies will live much longer...into the months and even years.

At four to seven days, the butterfly is mature enough to mate, which I have gone over in detail in the chapter on breeding butterflies.

The adult butterfly is a striking butterfly with deep orange wings that are outlined in black. White dots also cover the body and edges of the wings.

Although caterpillars feed on milkweed, adult monarch butterflies will feed on a range of flowers. They sip nectar through their proboscis, which a long coiled straw like tongue. They do not eat anything else as adults.

And that is the life cycle of the monarch butterfly. All butterfly species have the same lifecycle; however, the instars of the caterpillar will differ as will lifespan and the time it takes for metamorphosis.

5. Generations

As I mentioned at the beginning of this chapter, monarch butterflies have both stages of their lifecycle and generations. If you are not sure what a generation is, it refers to all the butterflies that are born around the same time. Monarch butterflies have a total of 4 generations born every year.

Every year, around February or March, the monarch butterflies that have been overwintering in the southern United States and Mexico come out of their period of diapauses, which is a type of reproductive hibernation.

When they come out, the adult monarchs begin mating before they start their migration north. The goal of this generation of monarch butterflies is to find milkweed plants for their larvae to eat. By March or April, the female monarch butterflies should have moved far enough north to find milkweed and they will lay their eggs on the milkweed they find. Those adult butterflies will die within 2 to 6 weeks after laying their eggs and their death will be the end of the fourth generation from the previous year.

The first generation for the current year will be hatched four days later. The caterpillar will be full grown within 2 weeks and will form a chrysalis, which will open to release the adult monarch butterfly 9 to 14 days after that.

Once this first generation reaches adulthood, they will continue north towards their summer homes.

After 4 to 7 days, the monarch butterflies are mature enough to mate and will do so. The females will search for a new place to lay eggs as they continue north.

When she finds a suitable place to lay her eggs, she will. Remember that each lifespan for a butterfly is between 2 to 6 weeks but can also be several months. For that reason, the butterfly may not die immediately after laying but may live for a few weeks after that.

The second generation of monarch butterflies hatch in March or June and the process will begin again with caterpillar to pupa to adult to breeding and laying adult. As the butterflies go through each generation, they are continually moving north as adult butterflies.

The third generation of monarch butterflies is born in July or August. Again, they follow the same development as the other two generations. They lay their eggs and it is the final generation, the fourth generation, that will live a slightly different life than the previous generations.

Although they do go through the same development as the previous generations, when they reach adulthood, they do not reach reproductive maturity 4 to 7 days after metamorphosis is complete. Instead, they will enter a reproduction diapauses, which will remain for 6 to 8 months.

The fourth generation is born in September or October, and will be adults before the first frost, which is when they will begin their migration south to their overwintering sites. Some of the fourth generation may be born in August, depending on the temperatures of the season but it is more commonly seen in early September.

Once they are adults, they will fly south and spend their winter in Mexico or Southern California. When winter is over, they will begin breeding and lay the eggs for the next first generation of the year.

6. Migration

Although migration can be covered elsewhere in this book, I want to take the time to go over it in this chapter. The main reason is that much of the migration is tied in with the generations of the monarch butterfly.

As you have seen in the generations, monarch butterflies go through four generations of butterflies each year. It is this fourth generation that will actually make the migration to and from Mexico. For this reason, the adult monarch butterfly from the fourth generation can live several months to several years, depending on the migratory pattern of that particular butterfly.

Although the monarch butterfly migrates both to and from Mexico, we always look at migration as starting on its migration back to Mexico. The fourth generation of monarch butterfly will enter what is known as a diapause, which is a type of hibernation where the butterfly will not breed.

During this stage, they will begin their migration, usually around August or September; however, they may not begin migration until the first frost occurs.

Where the monarchs migrate to depend on where they are located since they are spread out through much of North America. In the eastern populations, any population that is east of the Rocky Mountains, the monarch butterfly will migrate to Mexico, or specifically to the Trans-Mexican Volcanic Belt, which is home to pine-oak forests. Western populations, will move south down into California to spend their winters there.

In total, monarch butterflies will migrate up to 2500 miles and it is one of the longest insect migrations. In fact, only a few species of butterflies will migrate each year and in North America, it is only the monarch. Each year, the monarchs will return to the same trees and sanctuaries before starting their return trip north.

This return trip usually starts in February or March and it begins the reproductive system of the hibernating butterflies. During the trip north, several generations of monarchs will make the journey back to their summer homes as the butterflies will breed, lay eggs and the next generation will continue on.

Why do monarch butterflies migrate?

One of the biggest questions that people have around the monarch butterflies is why they migrate. There are actually three reasons for this.

First, the monarch butterfly migrates because it is too cold in their northern habitat. During the winter, the freezing temperatures are not hospitable for the monarch to survive. This means that the butterfly must move to warmer climates to ensure the next generation of monarchs.

Second, the food is sparse in wintering months and, depending on where the location is, it can be completely absent. Milkweed does not grow during winter months, which means that any eggs or larva produced in the northern climates, would not survive the winter.

Finally, they must make the return trip back to the north, since milkweed is not native to their overwintering sites. This means that they are unable to lay eggs in the southern locations so they have to travel to areas where milkweed flourishes.

Because of these three things, the monarch butterfly must make the journey to ensure their survival.

How do monarch butterflies migrate?

Although we know that monarch butterflies fly when they migrate, it is not clear how they find their way each year or even how they manage to survive the migration. Researchers have found that the monarch butterflies actually gain weight during their migration, which helps explain how the insect is able to sustain itself during the migration.

They have also found that monarchs will stop during their travel to collect nectar from flowering plants. They do not remain for long periods as they need to avoid cold weather. Monarch butterflies are cold blooded so they will not survive any cold temperatures. If they stop too long during their migration, they will end up succumbing to the cold.

In addition to getting their meals on the go, it is believed that monarch butterflies will ride the air waves to cut down on the amount of energy they expend in flight.

But how they find the exact same location as generations before them is a complete mystery since the butterflies that arrive in their summer or winter homes have never been there before. Studies are still being conducted on this but new research has shown that monarch butterflies use the earth's magnetic fields for orientation.

In fact, it is believed that there is an antenna, just a single antenna on the butterfly, that contains cryptochrome, which is a photoreceptor protein. The protein picks up the violet-blue light that allows the butterfly to determine how it is aligned with the magnetic field. Outside of that finding, it is still unclear how monarchs find their way each year.

One thing that I want to mention before closing off this chapter is that monarch butterflies can be found throughout the world. While they are primarily found in the America's, they have been found in Bermuda, Great Britain, Australia and New Zealand.

Although they have been located in various places, the monarch butterflies of North America are different in genetics from monarchs found elsewhere throughout the world, and this may be the reason why migration is primarily noted in these monarchs than in others.

Chapter 5. Risks to the Monarch Butterfly

If you have been reading any of the newspapers out there or listening to the news, you are probably aware of the fact that monarch butterflies are at risk. In fact, the populations are declining quite rapidly and many are emphasising the importance of conservation to stabilize the population.

While we cannot stop all of the factors that are affecting monarch butterflies today, there are things that we can do as an individual that will help us improve the health of the populations in our areas.

In this chapter, I will go over everything that you need to know about the risks, including diseases, that affect the monarch butterfly.

1. Environmental Risks

Although man is not a natural risk exactly, I have placed many of the things that affect the monarch butterfly population due to habitat destruction caused by man as an environmental impact on the monarch butterfly populations.

There are several different risks that are occurring with monarch butterflies and while we can help in some of the areas, there are things that we need long range plans to correct. In this section, I will go over both the environmental impact caused by man and the environmental impact that is not.

a) Loss of Habitat

When you ask any expert what the number one risk to monarch butterflies is, they will tell you loss of habitat. Every year, more and more fields of naturally blooming wild flowers are being destroyed for expansion of our city centers.

Many of the plants that monarch butterflies rely on for food are viewed as a weed and are targeted by herbicides when gardeners tend to their garden. This loss of habitat affects monarch butterflies in a large scale and without proper plants, the monarchs will not be able to lay their eggs and produce the next generation.

In addition to the loss of habitat in their summer ranges, monarch butterflies are also suffering from a loss of habitat in their overwintering home.

Although this loss is happening, many people have realized the importance of keeping these butterflies thriving and have begun to create butterfly friendly gardens. Cities, provinces and states have also begun to replant milkweed and goldenrod to provide monarchs with the foods they need throughout their life.

And you can create your own habitat for monarch butterflies, which I went over in creating a butterfly friendly garden.

b) Climate Change

As with other insects and animals around the world, climate change affects monarch butterflies significantly. If you have not read the chapter on migration, you may not be aware of the fact that monarch butterflies will migrate to Mexico and Southern California for the winter and then back up towards and into Canada for the summer months.

The butterflies know when this migration should occur because of the lengthening days and the cooler or warmer weather.

Unfortunately, with climate change, there are often sudden shifts of weather or summer arrives sooner in other countries than it does in northern climates. This means that the monarch butterfly may run into cold weather as they migrate north, which can kill them or a sudden drop in temperature that damages the butterflies and keeps them from migrating.

c) GMO Corn

This may seem surprising but GMO corn is a risk to monarch butterfly populations and to the population of many different insect species. The reason for

this is because GMO corn produces pollen that carries a toxin. This toxin kills pests that attack corn crops.

Unfortunately, the toxic pollen also covers many other plants and while it does attack pests, it also attacks many other insect populations including the monarch caterpillar.

While all life stages of butterfly are affected by this toxic pollen, it is the caterpillars that are at a higher risk of it. When the pollen leaves the corn plants, it often settles on milkweed, coating the leaves in a thick, yellow substance.

When the egg hatches, the monarch caterpillar begins eating its leaf and it eats the GMO pollen as it does. This pollen enters the caterpillar and the result is the death of the caterpillar.

The reason for this is that the toxin will enter the caterpillar and bind to specific sites in the caterpillar's stomach. When this happens, the wall of the gut becomes an open sieve and pathogens that are in the gut will spread through the body. It makes the caterpillar extremely sick until it dies.

With more and more GMO corn being used, the danger to monarch butterflies is increasing greatly. The result is a decrease in monarch butterfly populations.

As an individual, unless you are a farmer, there is very little that can be done on a large scale, however, speaking with your representative and signing petitions to stop the use of GMO will make an important impact in the survival of the monarch butterfly.

d) Pesticides and Herbicides

I have already mentioned these a bit but the use of both pesticides and herbicides are affecting monarch butterfly populations. Like the GMO corn pollen, pesticides and herbicides are indiscriminate. Herbicides attack the milkweed that caterpillars rely on and this results in the monarch butterfly not having anywhere to lay her eggs. In addition, it means that there is no food for the caterpillars.

Another problem is that many pesticides will attack both the adult monarch butterfly and the monarch butterfly during the larval stage. This lowers the population greatly and prevents new generations of monarch butterflies from hatching.

As you can see, while these things affect the environment of the monarch butterfly, there are many things that we can do to stop it. Plant monarch butterfly friendly gardens, reduce the use of pesticides and herbicides and also fight against climate change and the use of GMO corn.

2. Natural Predators

Although we want to help the populations of butterflies, we need to be aware of the fact that monarch butterflies do have natural predators. It is also important to note that natural predation, while fierce at times, is natural and it does not often affect the overall population in regards to size.

One thing that should be mentioned is that monarch butterflies are poisonous insects so many predators will leave them alone; however, there are a few predators that have built up a tolerance for the insects and will eat them on a regular basis.

a) Birds

Most birds will leave the monarch butterfly alone since the brightly colored butterfly and caterpillar warn predators that they are not appetizing in any way.

That being said, there are a number of birds that will eat the monarch butterfly in its adult stage. Predation of monarch butterflies is primarily seen in monarch butterflies during the winter months. There is some theory for this and many believe that the long migration, as well as the age of the monarchs, results in a lower amount of cardenolides in their system. This means that there is less chance of the bird getting sick when it eats the monarch butterfly.

While there are a number of birds that will try to eat a monarch, the two main birds that eat them are the following:

- **Black Beaked Oriole :** The black beaked oriole is a slim bird that grows to roughly 8 inches in size. It is one of the more common predators of the monarch butterfly and it resides in Mexico and Southern California where the monarchs overwinter.

  The black beaked oriole has a very unusual way of eating monarchs and will actually slit open the abdomen of the monarch prior to eating. This results in the contents of the monarch's abdomen to be removed and it is believed that the bird ends up eating less of the cadenolides that are in the digestive tract.

- **Black Headed Grosbeak:** The black headed grosbeak is a medium sized bird that primarily eats seeds but it will eat insects as well. It has a wide range in the Southwestern United States and into Mexico.

  While the black headed grosbeak does eat seeds, it accounts for a high level of monarch butterfly mortality. The bird does not eat the monarchs in any particular way, unlike the oriole, but it seems to have an immunity to the toxins in a monarch butterfly.

It is interesting to note that these two bird species account for roughly 60% of the mortality in monarch butterflies. It is also important to realize is that predation by these birds has actually increased due to environmental changes by man.

As forests are cut down, monarch butterflies have less habitat to overwinter in and the habitat that is left has less protection. This means that it is much easier for bird species, like the black headed grosbeak and the black beaked oriole, have more opportunity to hunt the monarch in mass.

b) Wasps

Wasps are a ferocious predator that will hunt a range of different insects. While they will attack adult monarch butterflies, the wasp is more likely to attack the caterpillar.

In winter, at the overwintering sites, there have been studies that show wasps attacking the full grown monarchs. This is seen more in California than in the overwintering sites in Mexico.   When the wasps do attack the monarch butterfly adult, they generally just feed on the abdomen of the butterfly.

In other areas, the wasps turn to feeding on the caterpillars. It is interesting to note that studies have shown that while the toxin in the caterpillars does not kill the wasps, it does affect their fertility rate. In addition, the wasps that do produce young end up producing deformed young. This abnormality is not seen in wasp colonies that do not feed on monarch caterpillars.

c) Spiders

Spiders are opportunistic feeders so they have been known to eat the occasional caterpillar or monarch butterfly that happens to get entangled in their hunting line.

Spider predation is rather minimal and to this date, there are no known spider species that hunt primarily on monarchs.

d) Ants

Another predator that has been seen attacking monarch butterflies is ants. Again, they are more likely to attack caterpillars but there have been some evidence of ants attacking adults, especially if that adult monarch butterfly is sick or injured.

In general, however, the ants focus primarily on monarch caterpillars and will attack them at any of the instar stages. They often swarm them in number to kill the caterpillar.

It is interesting to note that fire ants are one of the main predators of monarch caterpillars in some areas, specifically in Texas.

As you can see, there are not many predators that eat the monarch butterfly or its caterpillar but the predators that do can cause a significant amount of damage to the population.

3. Parasites and Other Risks

In addition to predation, there are a number of parasites that attack monarch butterflies, although the majority of these attack the young larva, there are some that attack at different stages of the monarch butterfly's development.

a) Fly Parasitoids

Although flies do not eat monarch butterflies or their larva, they do act as a parasite to the larva.

What this means is that when the larva hatch, they have immediate access to the host food and will begin to bore into the caterpillar.

One particular fly that attacks the monarch caterpillar is the La Fly. This is a fly that is very common in Brazil but it has also become prevalent in North and Central America. The La fly will place its eggs on the skin of the caterpillar.

When the eggs hatch, the La fly larvae bore into the body and continue developing. At first, the caterpillar does not seem to notice the infestation and will continue growing and developing. Near the end of the late larvae period or the early pupae period, the La fly maggots will erupt from the host and will begin dropping out of it. They drop to the ground using gelatinous tendrils that hang from the monarch caterpillar or pupa. The end result is the death of the monarch.

La flies are believed to affect roughly 13% of the monarch caterpillar population, which means that they do considerable damage to the population.

b) Wasp Parasitoids

Wasp parasitoids are also present as a parasite for the monarch butterfly and caterpillar. As we know, there are some populations of wasps that will eat the insects. However, there are several that will place their eggs onto the caterpillar so the larva can eat the host when they hatch.

Although it is unclear how many populations of wasps do this, research has shown that one wasp parasitoid that attacks the monarch pupa is the Chalcid wasp, which will lay its eggs into a developing pupa.

When the larva hatch, they feed on the pupa and then the wasps emerge. Up to 200 tiny wasps can emerge from one pupa.

There is no data on how frequently wasps affect monarch butterflies but we do know that they can have devastating effects on the population.

c) Fungi, Viruses and Bacteria

Another risk that is affecting the population of monarch butterflies is fungi, viruses and bacteria. Again, this is more commonly seen in the larval stage; however, it can also be seen in adults.

Generally, fungi, viruses and bacteria enter into the monarch's body orally as the monarch eats. This is one of the main reasons why it affects the caterpillar more than it does the adult monarch butterfly.

Once it has entered the body, the fungi, virus or bacteria begins to attack the caterpillar's body. This results in the caterpillar's internal organs shutting down and it will lead to death. Very few caterpillars survive infections from these invaders.

Again, there is little data about how frequently caterpillars and monarch butterflies succumb to these conditions but it is enough to make note of.

d) *Ophryocystis Elektroscirrha*

Also known commonly as OE, this condition is actually a protozoan parasite that is seen quite frequently in monarch and queen butterflies. The condition is caused by a single celled organism that is animal like in characteristic but is actually a parasite.

When the monarch butterfly is infected with the spores, she passes the protozoan onto her eggs and ultimately her larva. This leads to the caterpillar being infected; however it lives a host animal and does not appear overly affected by the spores. Instead, the spores go through their reproduction during the pupal stage, and this is where it affects the monarch butterfly the most.

Before we look closer at that, I wanted to look at the actual history of the protozoan. In reality, while it is a huge problem for monarch butterflies, the parasite was only first discovered in the 1960's. Before that time, it did not appear that

monarchs were affected by the spores at all. This suggests that the protozoan has evolved alongside the monarch butterfly since this species of butterfly seems to be the only one the spores attack.

When we are looking at the prevalence of this protozoan in monarch populations, studies have shown that the monarchs that migrate the farthest are less likely to care the spores.

In fact, when we look at the three populations of monarch butterflies in North America, it is the eastern population, which travels from Canada to Mexico every year that has the lowest percentage of infection by this parasite. Only 8% of the population is infected with it.

The populations that do not migrate, such as the monarch butterflies in Florida and Texas, have the highest population of OE infect monarchs. Up to 70% of the population is infected with the parasite.

Finally, the western population, which does migrate, albeit a shorter distance to Southern California, has an infection percentage of 30% of their population.

But what does OE mean to the monarch populations?

Well, the first thing is that OE spores are found on the outside of adult monarchs that have been infected. When they are on the infected adult monarch butterfly, the protozoan spore is actually a dormant cell. The host butterfly does not seem affected and the spores are so small that they are actually sandwiched between the scales on the butterfly.

As an infected adult, the monarch butterfly carries on with its natural instinct to breed and lay their eggs. However, it is the very act of egg laying that creates the most havoc in the process.

As the butterfly lays her egg, the spores that are lying dormant around her scales scatter over the egg and the surrounding milkweed leaves. This continues on with every egg that she lays.

When the caterpillar hatches, it eats its own shell and begins to eat the leaf around it. This means that the caterpillar has eaten the spores and it moves into the caterpillar's midgut.

Once it is there, the digestive juices of the caterpillar will begin to break down the spores. When it is broken down, the parasite will be released and it will move to the hypoderm in the intestinal wall.

After it is in the hypoderm, the OE protozoan will begin to reproduce asexually. What this means is that the protozoan parent will divide to increase the number of parasites in the caterpillar's body. This division can occur several times with each OE parent.

When the caterpillar goes into the pupal stage, the OE parasite will begin to reproduce sexually and this will create the spores that infect the monarch butterfly as an adult.

These spores will cover the adult butterfly when it emerges from the pupa. At that point, the spores will become dormant until the adult butterfly reproduces and lays eggs again.

Although it does not seem like an invasive parasite when you first think of them, OE is very serious and can be fatal to the monarch butterfly.

Generally, if the caterpillar is heavily infected with OE, the adult monarch may not emerge from the chrysalis. Those that do have a very difficult time emerging and often die in the process. Others will be so weak that they will fall off the pupal case and will be unable to expand their wings fully.

In addition, many of the monarchs emerge deformed and they will not survive very long either.

If the infection is mild, the adult monarch butterflies that are infected will often be much smaller than monarchs that are not infected. In addition, the forewings are often shorter due to the spores. Another side effect of this protozoan is damage to the outer layers of the monarch's abdomen. Then causes the butterfly to lose weight quickly and to dry out easily so the butterfly has to constantly eat and drink.

Infected monarch butterflies have more difficulty flying and males will usually be so weak that they will not search for a mate. Even when they find a receptive female, the infected male monarch butterfly is unable to mate or produce offspring.

As you can see, OE is devastating to the population of monarch butterflies and that is why more studies are being done on how to solve this problem.

And those are the conditions that you are going to see more commonly in monarchs. As you can see, while they are a fairly hardy butterfly, there are many things that are putting them at risk. While populations remain strong right now, studies are showing that this will not be the case for long.

Chapter 6. The Monarch Butterfly Friendly Yard

So you want to invite monarch butterflies into your yard. Well, that is a wonderful idea and one that can be done very easily without a lot of difficulty. In general, there are only a few things that you need to do in your yard and I will go over all of these things so you are sure to encourage monarch butterflies in your yard.

1. Tips and Guidelines

The very first thing that it is important to do is to follow a few guidelines for your garden. This will ensure that monarch butterflies find your yard and will ensure that they stay there to enjoy it.

Tip and Guideline Number 1: Look at your Yard

If you haven't already, make sure that you take a look at your yard with a discerning eye. Take note of the shade in your yard and also how much coverage your yard has. Although it may not seem like a huge deal, monarch butterflies need both sunlight and protection and it can be difficult finding just the right combination to attract your butterfly friends.

Tip and Guideline Number 2: Clear out the Shade

Although you will want to have protection for your monarch butterflies, you also want to give them plenty of sunlight to warm themselves. Remember, monarch butterflies are cold blooded and need sunlight to regulate their body temperature.

The ideal yard should have full sunlight between 10am and 3pm every day. This is the time when monarch butterflies are the most active so you want to make sure they get enough sunlight during that time.

Tip and Guideline Number 3: Plant a Treeline

If you don't have one to work with already, plant a treeline for your butterflies. This will create a natural wind break to ensure that the butterflies are protected from the wind. In addition, it will ensure that the butterflies have somewhere to hide in the event of a predator.

Tip and Guideline Number 3: Provide Water and Soil

Although monarch butterflies eat nectar, they do require water and some minerals so make sure that you have an area with access to water. In addition, provide areas where there is bare soil so the monarch butterflies can get sodium. Sodium is very important with breeding as males will transfer sodium to females during mating.

Tip and Guideline Number 5: Avoid Pesticides

Finally, make sure that you avoid spraying your yard with pesticides. While it may be tempting to fight predators and pests in your yard, pesticides do not discriminate and will kill any monarch butterflies that enter your yard. Since you want to make it a safe and friendly place for butterflies, avoid spraying.

Now that you have the general tips and guidelines, there is one last thing that you should remember and that is the plants. Make sure that you plant for every stage of your monarch butterflies life. I will go over plants for caterpillars and for adults in the next section.

2. Plants for Caterpillars

As you know, monarch butterflies, specifically the young, need specific plants to survive. Adult monarch butterflies will lay their eggs on milkweed plants and the larvae of the monarch butterfly will eat it.

Although many people view milkweed as a weed, it is actually a wildflower that is found in many areas. While we often think of milkweed the same, there are actually over 2000 species of milkweed. The majority of milkweed species are found in Africa and South America. In addition, while most monarch butterflies lay on milkweed that thrives in Canada, with the exception of Newfoundland and Labrador, they will lay on many different species of milkweed.

When you are choosing plants for your garden, it is important to plant milkweed. The reason for this is so that the butterflies will want to lay their eggs in your garden. When there is a food source for their larvae, the monarch butterfly will stay in your garden instead of venturing out to search for food.

While I strongly recommend planting milkweed, make sure that you only plant milkweed that is found in your area. Do not introduce a new species as the milkweed will begin to spread.

Finally, be prepared for that milkweed to last. Milkweed is a perennial wildflower so once you plant it; you will see it year after year so make sure you are committed to the butterfly garden.

Although there are 2000 species of milkweed available to plant, there are four milkweed species that are commonly found in North America and I will go over each of them.

a) Common Milkweed

Common milkweed is a wildflower with drooping flowers of pink, white or lavender. The flowers are rounded and usually grow in clusters. The leaves of the common milkweed plant are oblong in shape and should have a green topside with a woolly, grey underside. The seed pods of the common milkweed should be greyish green with a warty appearance.

Common milkweed blooms between June and early August and the seed pods form in late August to September.

When planting, common milkweed prefers rocky flat areas that have good irrigation but I do not recommend this plant for a regular backyard. This is better to have in a large acreage as it is very invasive and will quickly take over a yard. One recommendation that I can give you is to plant it in ditches near your yard. You can draw the adult butterflies into your yard for food and provide them with plants for their eggs and larva without having the plant invade your yard too much.

b) Butterfly Milkweed

Butterfly milkweed is a more common milkweed that you can see in smaller gardens. Again, remember that it does spread, however, not as invasively as common milkweed. The butterfly milkweed produces  clusters of red, orange or yellow flowers, although orange is the most common. It should have an oblong shape to the leaves and the long, greed seedpods should be tapered at both ends.

While it does attract monarch butterflies, it should be noted that it does not produce the milky juice that is seen in other species of milkweed.

The plant does very well in dry soil and can thrive in partial to full sunlight. It is commonly seen in prairies so it is quite a hardy perennial plant. It blooms in June to September and should only be planted in the fall.

One precaution with this milkweed is that it is poisonous to livestock and other animals so if you have pets that will be in your garden, make sure you plant your milkweed where your pets can't reach it.

c) Swamp Milkweed

Another milkweed that is not good for every yard, swamp milkweed prefers standing water and moist, fully saturated soil. It is a perfect plant if you have some type of pond or water feature in your yard since it needs moisture to thrive. It is a pretty milkweed that has pink, almost flesh-colored clusters of flowers with a distinct hood and horn structure to the flower.

The plant blooms from June to August and the seed pods, which are tapered at both ends and have a slender shape, mature between late August and October. The plant is quite short compared to other milkweed varieties.

The plant does need full sun for proper growth so it is important to provide the plant with both water and light.

d) Poke Milkweed

The final type of milkweed that you can offer to any monarchs that come in your yard is poke milkweed. This milkweed has flowers that are clustered together loosely and are white in coloring. One of the interesting properties of this plant is that it is often tinted green or lavender. The green leaves are oblong in shape and the seed pods are long and tapered at both ends.

Poke milkweed blooms from June to August and the seeds mature between August and October. They do well in full or partial shade but need a rich soil. The plant is often found at the edge of woods and forests.

Remember that all species of milkweed are a wildflower so they spread very easily. Be sure to watch your milkweed and stop it from spreading as soon as you see new shoots. Also, it is important to note  that milkweed can cause allergic reactions in people so be thoughtful of any neighbors.

By having these plants in or near your yard, you are providing habitat for your monarch butterflies and this will ensure that they lay in their eggs where you can enjoy them.

3. Plants for Monarch Butterflies

Now that we have gone over the plants the caterpillars will be eating, it is time to look at the plants that the adult monarch butterflies will be eating.

Unlike caterpillars, monarch butterflies enjoy a range of different nectars from flowers and do not rely on milkweed as a food source. What this means for you is that you can have a range of food for your monarch butterflies without having to rely too heavily on plants that are invasive.

One thing to pay attention to in your garden is with having fall wildflowers in your garden. Although monarch butterflies will drink nectar from a range of plant species, it is the fall wildflowers that give them the nutrients they need for migration. If you do not live near any areas that are natural habitats for these fall wildflowers, then it is important to plant them in your garden

a) Boneset

A flower that blooms from July to September, the boneset is a plant that has tall stems and hairy, lance shaped green leaves. The plant should have clusters of white florets

on the top of the stems.

Commonly found in meadows and fields, the boneset can do well in any type of yard that has moist soil and lots of sunlight. They do not require a lot of care to grow and once they are in a yard, it can be difficult to remove them from a planter.

b) Goldenrod

Known as a common weed, goldenrod is actually a food that is important to monarch butterflies. It provides them with much of the nutrients they need to migrate. Unfortunately, it is being attacked with herbicides as most people feel that this plant is nothing more than a vile weed.

That being said, goldenrod is an important plant to have for your monarch butterfly gardens. The plant is a tall plant that has canoe shaped leaves that have a coarse tooth like shape to them. At the top of the stalks there are arching branches that have tiny yellow flowers on top of them.

Goldenrod thrives in a variety of habitats from dry fields to moist floodplains. They do require average moisture levels but they can survive drought like conditions at times. In addition, they can do well in full to partial sun.

One thing that should be noted is that goldenrod does not cause hay fever. That is actually a myth and a misconception about the plant. Another important point that should be mentioned is that both honeybees, which are very important to pollination, and butterflies thrive with this plant that blooms between May and September.

c) Black-Eyed Susan

One of my favorite flowers, black eyed Susan is a yellow daisy like flower with a black or brown disks in the center. The plant has oblong shaped leaves that are slightly toothed and they only grow to about 35 inches in height so they are not the largest wildflower that you can choose for your garden.

This plant, which blooms between June to September, does very well in any type of garden and can thrive in both full sunlight and partial shade. It is important to realize that Black-eyed Susans are an invasive flower that will spread quickly so only plant it in areas where it is native.

d) **Wild Bergamot**

Wild bergamot is a pale violet wildflower that grows in clusters at the end of a branchlike plant. The leaves are lance shaped and should be long with a light green. The plant is actually very pleasing to have in  the yard because the violet flowers are very beautiful and the plant itself has a mint-like scent to it.

The plant does require good drainage, although the soil should be slightly moist. It can do well in full sunlight but remember that this is a larger plant and will take up room in your garden.

e) **New England Aster**

 New England Aster is a pretty wildflower that has clusters of flowers on branchlike stems. The plant can grow up to a metre in height and has long leaves that attach to long, hairy stems. The flowers of the New England Aster are a

rosy lilac to deep purple in color. The large clusters of flowers should have yellow to orange centers in each of the flower.

The plant does well in moist soil and can have full to partial sun. It can be one of the more difficult flowers to grow, especially for a first time plant, but once it is established, it is a very hardy perennial. The plant blooms between August to October.

f) Common Yarrow

The final flower that we will be looking at for your monarch butterfly friendly yard is the common yarrow. This plant has leaves that look very similar to a carrot leaf and they are actually quite feathery in appearance. The flowers should form flat clusters on the stem ends and should be white or yellow.

The clusters should be quite dense.

The flower blooms between June and August. It requires full to partial sunlight and a rich, moist soil to grow. The smell of the plant is quite pungent so you may want to avoid having it grow around eating and seating areas in your garden.

And there you have it. If you plant a nice blend of the flowers explained in this chapter, and follow the guidelines, you are sure to have a monarch butterfly friendly yard.

Chapter 7. Raising Monarch Butterflies for Conservation

As you may have realized, the last chapter is an excellent way for you to boost the population of monarch butterflies since you are providing natural habitat for them. If you have not read the chapter on risks to the monarch butterfly, be sure to read it. Habitat destruction is one of the major problems that are affecting monarch butterfly populations.

While many people are choosing to create a monarch butterfly friendly yard, many people are going further and rearing monarch butterflies themselves.

Although this can be a challenge, if you have the proper tools to do so, you can aid monarch butterflies through breed and release programs. Unlike mammals and birds, raising a butterfly in captivity will not affect any of its natural instincts to migrate.

In this chapter, I will go over everything you need to know about raising and rearing monarch butterflies in captivity.

1. Important Rules

Before we get into the steps to rearing monarch butterflies, I want to take a moment to go over a few important rules that you should follow. These will ensure that your populations remain healthy and that you do not create a population that is infected by the OE parasite. If you are not aware of what the OE parasite is, please read the chapter on risks to monarch butterflies.

One thing that I want to stress is that you do not need a huge set up to properly raise monarch butterflies. In general, caterpillars don't take much room and if you are releasing the adults, you can use small butterfly rearing kits. If you are releasing them into a greenhouse setting, you will need to make sure that all of their plant foods are available and you will have to pay special care to the temperature. Finally, make sure that you set up a special area for the butterflies to reach that contains milkweed so you have an easier time finding the eggs and placing them into their containers.

Please read the chapter on getting to know the monarch butterfly to understand what types of food they like through all the stages.

Tip Number 1: Keep things Sterilized

The very first tip that I stress is that you need to keep things sterilized. Everything that you will be using to raise your monarch butterflies, including the flight cages, containers, butterfly nets and the area that they are being raised, should be sterilized.

To do this, create a bleach solution of 20% bleach and 80% water. Once you have the solution, spray down the counters and then soak all of the plastic and fabric in the solution. You want to leave them at least 4 hours but it is better to let them soak overnight to ensure that you have killed any possible spores, fungi, bacteria or viruses.

Allow them to air dry and keep them separate from your current butterfly populations if you are not using them.

On a daily basis, make sure you wash down any counters that may have come into contact with any other butterflies or things that can be infected.

By being careful with sterilization, you are less likely to spread any diseases or the OE parasite if you have an infected caterpillar or butterfly.

Tip Number Two: Use Sterilized Milkweed

When you are feeding your monarch caterpillars, it is important to only used sterilized milkweed. This will lower the risk of any type of parasite getting through to your monarch caterpillars.

The best way to sterilize your milkweed is to soak it in a bleach solution. Since the milkweed is going to be eaten, you only want to use a 10% bleach solution. Also, only soak it for 20 minutes.

Once it is bleached, run it under water until all of the solution is off of it. If you forget this step, you could kill your caterpillars.

Tip Number Three: Grow your Own Milkweed

If you have the facilities to do so, set up a small greenhouse to grow your own milkweed. The reason why I recommend this is because you will not have to use wild milkweed to feed your caterpillars. This means a lower risk of giving them milkweed that is infected with parasites.

If you do grow your own milkweed, grow it indoors. Even if you are sure that the populations of monarch butterflies in your area are free of OE, even one infected milkweed leaf can infect your entire population.

Tip Number Four: Wear Disposable Gloves

Another important step to keeping your monarch butterflies healthy is to wear disposable gloves whenever you are working with the butterfly or their larva. In fact, I recommend that you wear disposable gloves whenever you have to do anything with your caterpillars.

Tip Number Five: Don't Overcrowd

When you are setting up your containers for your monarch caterpillars, it is important to avoid overcrowding your larvae. Never have more than 10 caterpillars in a 2 x 2 plastic container with a mesh lid.

The best though is to use a slightly smaller container and only house one caterpillar per container. This will ensure that you are not spreading the disease.

And those are the tips that you should follow. Remember that keeping a clean environment, plenty of food and just the right amount of space will ensure that your caterpillars grow well.

2. Determining Gender

When it comes to gender, you will not be able to determine it with eggs or with caterpillars. However, gender can be determined quite easily with monarch butterfly adults. The reason for this is that males have a few distinct features from females and it makes sex selection much easier.

These features are:

Feature Number One: Brighter Colors

While monarch butterflies of both sexes have a vibrant orange coloration to their wings, the female monarch butterfly actually has a brighter orange than the male. The male monarch butterfly has a brownish orange coloration.

Feature Number Two: Two Black Dots on the Hindwings

Another feature that you will see on a male butterfly is a single black dot near the bottom of each hindwing. Female butterflies do not have this trait and it is actually the Androconia Scales that have the pheromone sacks under them. The black dots are center of the hindwing but near the bottom.

Feature Number Three: Dark Webbing

On the wings of any monarch butterfly, there is a dark webbing that creates panels of color. The webbing outlines the orange and is actually the veins in the wings. While most people don't notice it, male monarch butterflies have thinner webbing than females. Females have dark, thick webbing.

Feature Number Four: Claspers on the end of the Abdomen

The final feature that you can use to tell the difference between a male and female monarch butterfly is the presence of claspers on the abdomen, at the bottom. These claspers are only seen on males and are used for gripping the female during mating.

While the differences may not seem huge, you will quickly see that the differences between a male and female monarch butterfly is greatly different when you know what to look for.

3. Breeding Monarch Butterflies

When it comes to breeding monarch butterflies, there really isn't a lot that you need to do except provide them with the proper environment. The butterflies will do the rest.

As I have mentioned in the chapter on the lifecycle of the monarch butterfly, the adult monarch butterfly is ready to breed within 4 to 7 days after they have emerged from the pupa.

a) Eggs

If you are just starting out, there are actually two different ways that you can collect your eggs. First, you could purchase the eggs from butterfly supply service. This can be an easy way to start but it can be difficult to determine if the caterpillar has OE or not.

The other way is to collect eggs from outside. Since monarch butterfly eggs are single eggs on milkweed leaves, it can be quite easy to find them. Search through milkweed patches carefully and when you locate any eggs, carefully take the entire leaf.

You will not be able to screen for OE so keep the leaf separate from other eggs. Make sure you label when you collected the egg and where you collected it from when you set up the containers.

After that, it is just a matter of waiting for the eggs to hatch.

b) Caterpillar

Once your egg hatches, you will be left with your caterpillar. This can be very exciting as you get to watch your caterpillar go through the 5 instars of development.

Once your caterpillar is hatched, you should give the caterpillar fresh milkweed on a daily basis. Since the plant is not growing with the caterpillar, it will lead to the leaves drying out quickly.

The caterpillar gets all of its moisture, nutrients and food from the milkweed leaves so keeping them fresh will ensure that the caterpillar is getting everything it needs.

Another thing that you should do every few days is to properly clean and sterilize the containers. Place the caterpillar into a clean, sterilized container while you work. When you are doing this, take the time to look over the caterpillar to make sure that it is healthy. If you see any signs of disease, remove the caterpillar from your program.

After about 2 weeks, the caterpillar will turn into a pupa. At this point, there is nothing that you need to do except watch your pupa transform.

c) Pupa

As I mentioned, there really isn't a lot that you need to do. Keep a close eye on your pupa to make sure that it doesn't turn brown. If it turns brown or black, there is a very good chance that the caterpillar has OE and you do not want it emerging around your other pupa.

Instead, remove it and monitor it elsewhere. One thing that should be noted is that the pupa will have a brown appearance shortly before the butterfly emerges. The reason for this is because what you are actually seeing is the monarch butterfly. The pupa itself is transparent.

d) The Adult

After 9 to 14 days, your adult monarch butterfly will begin emerging from the pupa. This is a very exciting time for everyone and it can be very tempting to help your monarch butterflies out of their pupa.

DON'T! The process of struggling out of the pupa is very important for monarch butterflies to properly stimulate their system. If you help them, their wings may not dry properly and may remain crumpled after drying.

Instead, just watch them and allow them to stay in the container for about 8 hours. This will give them ample time to dry out and be ready to take flight.

Once they are dry, you can carefully transfer them to their new greenhouse home or your butterfly cage. Be sure to monitor your butterflies and if you see any sign of OE, remove that butterfly from your population.

If you are releasing them, only release them during warmer weather. Never release them in winter, even if you climate is mild as there may not be enough food for them to survive, even if the days stay warm.

After about 4 to 7 days, your butterflies will begin breeding on their own and the cycle will start again.

4. Problems for Breeders

Although the problems seen are often the result of OE or other parasite, there are some things that may happen even to healthy populations. Before I close this chapter, I want to look at these problems.

a) Caterpillar Death

Even in the healthiest of populations, you will see the death of caterpillars. If you remember back to the lifecycle, many caterpillars will die when they have their first meal of milkweed. Others contract fungi, bacteria or parasites other than OE.

It is important to note that there are signs that your caterpillar is sick. These are:

1. The caterpillar stops eating and instead of shedding its skin, it begins to shrink and wither.

2. The caterpillar turns black.

3. The caterpillar will become mush instead of a pupa after the 5th instar.

4. The caterpillar will fall to the bottom of the container and remain there.

5. You may see some parasites.

If you find that your caterpillar did die, remove it immediately and also remove all of the milkweed. Transfer the healthy caterpillars to a sterile container and give them fresh milkweed. Throw out the old milkweed and sterilize the container for future use.

b) Adult Death

As with caterpillars, you will see mortality in your adult monarch butterflies, however, that is usually due to mismanagement.

When you start to see your monarch butterflies dyeing, it is very important to really look at your population. They may die because of the following:

1. Temperatures are too high. Too much heat will dehydrate your butterflies and can lead to their death.

2. No access to water. Remember that butterflies do not live solely on nectar so make sure that they have fresh water daily.

3. Temperature is too cold. Although short periods of cold temperatures are okay, if there is a constant low temperature, the health of your butterflies can be at risk.

4. Butterflies are starving. On a regular basis, check the size of your monarch butterfly's abdomen. If it is plump, the butterfly is getting enough to eat. If it is thin, it is starving. To correct this, provide ample food for your butterflies.

By being aware of your populations, you can prevent many diseases and create a healthy generation of monarch butterflies.

Chapter 8. Resources

The final points that I want to go over, before we look at common terms you should expect in the butterfly world, I wanted to give you a list of resources that every monarch butterfly enthusiast should be aware of.

1. Conservation and Health

Below are a list of organizations that are working towards the health and conservation of monarch butterflies.

- Monarch Alert:
  http://monarchalert.calpoly.edu

- Journey North:
  http://www.learner.org/jnorth/monarch

- Monarch Health:
  http://www.monarchparasites.org

- Cibolo Nature Center: http://www.cibolo.org

- Wild Ones: Native Plants, Natural Landscapes:
  http://www.wildones.org

- The Monarch Joint Venture,
  http://www.monarchjointventure.org

- University of Minnesota Monarch Lab,
  http://www.monarchlab.org

- The Xerces Society for Invertebrate
  Conservation: http://www.xerces.org

- North American Butterfly Association:
  http://naba.org

- Monarch Watch:
  http://www.monarchwatch.org

- Iowa Department of Natural Resources Prairie
  Resource Center:
  http://www.iowadnr.gov/Environment/LandSt
  ewardship/PrairieResourceCenter.aspx

- Southwest Monarch Study:
  http://www.swmonarchs.org

- Monarch Butterfly Fund:
  http://www.monarchbutterflyfund.org

- Pollinator Partnership:
  http://www.pollinator.org

- U.S. Fish and Wildlife Service:
  http://www.fws.gov

- The Reppert Lab: http://reppertlab.org

2. Resources for Education about Monarch Butterflies

These are interesting resources that will help spread awareness and education about monarch butterflies.

- Wild for Monarchs Campaign:
  http://www.wildones.org/land/monarch

- Flight of the Butterflies:
  http://www.flightofthebutterflies.com

- Pollinator LIVE: A Distance Learning Adventure:
  http://www.pollinatorlive.pwnet.org

3. Butterfly Gardening

Interested in raising a beautiful garden for butterflies, including the monarch butterfly to enjoy? These resources will help:

- The Butterfly Site:
  http://www.thebutterflysite.com/gardening.shtml

- Monarch Butterfly Garden:
  http://www.monarchbutterflygarden.net/butterfly-garden-resources

- Lady Bird Johnson Wildflower Center:
  http://www.wildflower.org/ladybird

4. Milkweed Resources

While it is important to learn as much as you can about monarch butterflies, it is just as important to learn what you can about milkweed.

- Western Monarch Milkweed Survey:
  http://www.xerces.org/milkweedsurvey

- Biota of North America's Asclepias Page:
  http://www.bonap.org/BONAPmaps2010/Ascl
  epias.html

- USDA Plants Asclepias Profile:
  http://plants.usda.gov/core/profile?symbol=A
  SCLE

- Monarchs and milkweeds:
  http://www.treesearch.fs.fed.us/pubs/43796

Chapter 9. Common Terms

Throughout this book, I have used a range of terms to discuss the Monarch Butterfly and butterflies in general. While many of the terms are common, it is important for anyone interested in butterflies to have an understanding of the common terms used by those who enjoy watching these wonderful little insects.

Abdomen: In connection with butterflies, the abdomen refers to the last part of the body that is found directly behind the thorax.

Aberration: Referring to an abnormal phenotype in the butterfly, usually found in coloration or the wing pattern, that is caused by a range of factors including environmental, genetic or development causes.

Adaptation: Referring to any feature or characteristic on a butterfly that has changed by natural selection to function better in that butterflies environment.

Adult: The final stage of the butterfly life cycle. This can range in length depending on the species but with butterflies, the average adult lifespan is between 2 to 6 weeks and some can live up to 8 months.

Aedeagus: Referring to the male reproductive organ, it is an intromittent organ that is used to deliver sperm.

Alkaloids: A plant compound that is believed to be an important factor in the host-plant selection of butterflies.

Allochronic: Referring to a butterfly that is active in different seasons.

Allopatric: Butterfly populations that have similar features but occur in different areas.

Anal Angle: A term referring to the enclosed area around the anus that is enclosed by the inner and outer margins of the hindwing.

Anal Fold: The fold on the inner margin of the hindwing.

Annellus: A sheath that is enclosed in the aedeagus.

Androconium: A scale that is found on the wings of some male butterflies that is known to secrete a pheromone.

Annulated: Usually used in reference to the antennae, this is a term referring to the ring like segments on the butterfly.

Antenna: The long, appendage on the butterfly's head. Butterflies have two.

Apical: A term that refers to the spot of wing that is near the tip of the wing.

Apiculus: The part of the antenna that is hooked.

Aposematism: Referring to the bright, contrasting colors found on insects. These colors are used to tell predators that the insect, such as the butterfly or caterpillar is unpalatable.

Areole: A small window, or subdivision, at the base of the wing scale.

Automimicry: When an insect bears the resemblance to another insect that is unpalatable to predators.

Band: The line of color found on caterpillars that run from the dorsal to ventral sides.

Basad: The area that is found towards the wing base.

Basking: When a butterfly spends time in the sunlight. This is used for thermoregulation.

Batesian Mimicry: When an insect bears the resemblance to another insect that is unpalatable to predators.

Biennial: A butterfly that has a two year cycle.

Bilaterial Gynandromorph: A butterfly that has male and female characteristics, however, these characteristics are found on one side. For instance, one side of the butterfly is male and the other side is female.

Bivoltine: A butterfly that has two flights per year.

Brood: A single generation of butterflies that emerge as adults at roughly the same time.

Bursa Copulatrix: A sac that is found in the abdomen of female butterflies. This is where spermatophors are stored.

Cardenolides: A plant compound that creates a defense against predators in the insects that eat the plant. Commonly found in milkweed.

Caterpillar: A juvenile larva of the butterfly.

Cell: Any part of the wing that is surrounded by veins.

Cervical Shield: Found in caterpillars, it is a sclerotized area behind the head that is heavily pigmented.

Chevron: A term that refers to a colored mark on a caterpillar that is shaped like a "V".

Chorion: The shell of the butterfly egg.

Chrysalis: The hard casing that a caterpillar creates around itself while it is transforming into a butterfly. Also known as a pupa.

Cilia: Referring to the fine hairs that are found on the edges of the wing.

Clade: Referring to a butterfly species that is descended from a single species.

Cline: The gradual progression of changes in physical characteristics in butterflies, usually as a result of geographic ranges.

Club: The thick portion of the butterfly's antenna.

Clypeus: This is the plate that is found on the bottom front of the head, just below the antenna.

Collar: The plate, which is a dorsal plate, that is found behind the head of the caterpillar.

Colony: This term is used to describe a population of butterflies that is maintained for a number of years.

Cogeneric: Butterflies that belong to the same genus.

Conspecific: Butterflies that belong to the same species.

Costa: The veining that is found on the edge of the wings. Used to heavily reinforce the wing.

Costal Fold: A flap on the forewing that contains scent scales. Commonly found in male butterflies, they can also be found in some females.

Costal Margin: The area of the wing that is found close to the Costa.

Coxa: The part of the leg that is found near the body of the butterfly.

Cremaster: Found on butterfly pupa, it is a hook like structure that is used to anchor the caterpillar into a silken pad.

Crenulate: Anything that is scalloped.

Crepuscular: A term referring to any butterfly that is more active during periods of dim light such as at dusk.

Crochets: Seen on certain species of butterflies, they are tiny hooks that are found on the prolegs of larvae.

Crypsis: Coloration that serves as a camouflage.

Cubital: A term used to refer to the veins in the wings.

Deme: When a population of butterflies are the result of interbreeding.

Diapause: A term that refers to a type of hibernation or dormancy in butterflies that is more commonly caused by a developmental arrest.

Dimorphism: When a species of butterfly has two distinct forms in the same population. For example, when males have a distinct difference from female butterflies.

Discal: The portion of the win that runs from the costa to the inner wing, it should be located in the central wing.

Discal Cell: A cell that extends from the base of the wing to the center.

Dorsal: The upper or top surface of the wing. It is commonly seen when the butterfly holds the wing open.

Dorsal-Basking: When a butterfly spends time in the sunlight with its wings open broadly. This is used for thermoregulation.

Dorsal Nectary Organ: Found in larvae, it is a gland in the 7th abdominal segment that produces a sweet substance that is attractive to ants.

Ecdysis: A term used to describe the molting or shedding that is done when a caterpillar sheds its skin.

Eclosion: When an adult butterfly emerges from its chrysalis.

Egg: The initial life stage of butterflies, eggs are laid by adult butterflies and hatch into caterpillars.

Endemic: Referring to a species of butterfly, or even a population, that is limited to a specific and restricted geographic area.

Endophagous: A caterpillar that feeds internally in a plant to conceal itself from a predator.

Epiphysis: A process of the butterfly that is used to clean the antenna.

Estivation: A type of hibernation or dormancy that is caused by summer heat or drought.

Evolution: The genetic change of a species over time due to natural selection.

Exophagous: A caterpillar that feeds externally in a plant to conceal itself from a predator.

Extant: Referring to butterflies that are still in existence.

Extinct: A butterfly that has no living representations alive today.

Extirpated: A butterfly that is still living but has become extinct in a specific location.

Exuvium: Referring to the skin of the larvae that is shed.

Eyespot: Markings on the wings that resemble an eye.

Family: This is a grouping of butterflies in the Linnaean system. Butterflies have six families in North and Central America and the Monarch Butterfly belongs to the Nymphalidae family.

Femur: The third section of the leg, this is found between the trochanter and tibia.

Filaments: The appendages that are found on caterpillars.

Flagellum: A term referring to the distal segment, which is found in the antenna of butterflies.

Flight: Refers to one generation of adults.

Flight Period: Refers to the span of time when adult butterflies can be found.

Forewing: The front wings on an insect.

Frass: The droppings of a caterpillar; also known as excrement.

Frons: The hair like tufts that are found between the eyes of the butterfly. It can also refer to the area between the eyes whether there is a tuft of hair or not.

Generation: The life cycle of all the individuals in a butterfly population.

Genitalia: This term is used in reference to the sexual, reproductive organs of adult butterflies.

Genus: The rank of the butterfly in the Linnaean system.

Geographic Specification: When there is an

isolation of two or more populations that results in a species level taxa.

Girdle: The thread that supports the middle of the chrysalis.

Granulosis: A disease that affects the larvae of butterflies.

Gravid: Refers to a female butterfly that is carrying eggs.

Gulching: Referring to a behavior that male butterflies do to search for receptive females.

Gynandromorph: A butterfly that has male and female characteristics.

Hair Pencils: Hairs that are found on the legs. They are believed to aid in spreading pheromones.

Hemolymph: The "blood" of insects, including butterflies.

Hibernaculum: The winter shelter of a butterfly.

Hibernation: A dormancy during the winter months.

Hilltopping: Referring to a behavior where the males of butterflies will stay on hilltops in search of receptive females.

Hindwing: The rear wings of an insect.

Holometabolous: Refers to any insect, such as a Monarch Butterfly, that goes through a complete metamorphosis.

Honeydew: A liquid that is excreted by some butterfly larvae as a by-product of their food. The liquid is very sweet.

Hyaline Spots: Glass like spots on a butterfly's wings that are translucent.

Imaginal Discs: These are clusters of embryonic cells that help produce the adult stage.

Imago: Another term used to describe an adult butterfly.

Inclusion-body Diseases: A term used to identify viruses that affect the protein crystals in the body. The diseases affect caterpillars.

Influx Species: A species of butterfly that enters into a region from a different region annually. Monarch Butterflies are an influx species.

Infuscated: A butterfly that is shaded with black or gray.

Instar: This term refers to the period between molts of the caterpillar.

Irruptive: Referring to a species of butterfly that will invade an distant area from where it resides.

Johnston's Organ: A sensory organ that is found in the second segment of the antenna. It is used to detect movements or vibrations.

Juxta: The male genitalia.

Labial Palp: Two structures that are found on either side of the proboscis in adult butterflies. The structure serves as a sensory function.

Lamella Antevaginalis: The female butterflies genitalia that are located anterior.

Lamella Postvaginalis: The female butterflies genitalia that is located posterior.

Larva: The young of a butterfly, also known as a caterpillar.

Larval Foodplant: This is a term used to describe any type of plant that is eaten by caterpillars. It is commonly where eggs are laid.

Lateral Basking: When a butterfly spends time in the sunlight but only turns one wing or one side of its body to the sun. The wings are closed when the butterfly is doing lateral basking. This is used for thermoregulation.

Lek: Referring to an area where males congregate to attract female butterflies.

Lebidoptera: The second largest order of insects, which butterflies are a part of.

Lepidopterology: The study of butterflies.

Local: The population of butterflies found in a geographical area.

Lunule: Crescent shaped marks that are found on the wings of some butterflies.

Marginal: Referring to the outer edge of the wing.

Mate-locating Behavior: Behavior seen in butterflies to find and attract a mate.

Maxillary Galea: The elongated structures that are found in adult butterflies. They should form the proboscis.

Meconium: Waste product that is caused by the metamorphosis. It is usually red in coloration.

Medial Vein: The vein found in the fourth wing.

Median: A term used to refer to the area located between the base and the apex; it should be at the very center.

Mediobasal: The line that is found in the basal area. It should be the central transverse line.

Mediodiscal: The line that is found on the wing, which bisects the discal area. It should be a central transverse line.

Melanic: A butterfly that has a dark or blackish coloration, which is darker than the species.

Mesothorax: The middle section of the thorax.

Metapopulation: A set of butterfly populations that occasionally exchange genes or individuals between them.

Metathorax: The third section of the thorax.

Migration: Term used to describe a movement of organisms from one location to another, usually, migrations are seasonal.

Mimicry: When an insect bears the resemblance to another insect that is unpalatable to predators.

Molt: The term referring to the shedding of the larval skin.

Monandry: When a butterfly female only mates with one male.

Monophagous: A species of butterfly that has specialized larvae when it comes to food plant choices.

Morph: Any individual form that is found in a polymorphic species.

Multivoltine: Any butterfly species that has three or more flights per year.

Naturalized: Any type of butterfly that is sustaining its population in a new environment without human assistance.

Nectaring: Feeding on the nectar of flowering plants.

Nest: A structure made of leaves, silk and other debris that is made by caterpillars to hide.

Nudum: The scaleless area on the tip of the antenna.

Nuptial Gifts: Nutrients that a male butterfly transfers to a female during mating. This is only seen in some butterfly species.

Obtect: Rounded

Oligophagous: A caterpillar that feeds on foodplant from only a few plant species.

Ommatidium: Referring to the eye of the larva.

Ommatidium: Referring to each facet of the adult eye.

Order: The rank of an insect in the Linnaean system.

Osmeterium: The gland that is found on the first segment of a caterpillar. It is a fleshy gland that secrets a defensive liquid with a pungent odor.

Overwintering Stage: A stage of the butterfly lifecycle that hibernates through the winter. It is different for every species of butterfly with some overwintering stages being during the egg stage, others during the caterpillar and so on.

Oviposit: Laying one or more eggs.

Ovipositor: The structure found on the tip of the abdomen in female butterflies. This is where the eggs are laid.

Ovum: The egg.

Panmictic: Populations that are of interbreeding with populations from all of the parts of their range.

Parasitoid: A free living adult that has a larval stage that feeds on a single host such as a butterfly.

Partial Flight: Refers to a population of adults that emerged from the pupa stage while a portion of the population remains dormant in their chrysalis.

Patrolling: A mating behavior seen in male butterflies where they will fly long distances to find a receptive female.

Pedicel: The second segment found in the antenna.

Perching: A mating behavior seen in male butterflies where they will wait in one spot until a receptive female flies by.

Pharate Adult: The stage of a butterfly's lifecycle where you can see the fully formed adult in the pupal casing right before emergence.

Phenotype: The differences in an adult due to a particular characteristic.

«Pheromone: A secretion from one organism that creates behavioral changes in another organism from the same species.

Phylogeny: The line of descent for an organism.

Population: This is a term that refers to a group of butterflies that belong to the same species in a defined geographical area.

Postbasal: The part of the wing that is just below the base.

Postdiscal Band: The band that is seen on some butterfly wings that lies between the discal and submarginal areas.

Postmedian: The area of the wing around the central portion of the wing.

Prepupal: This is the stage in the larval lifecycle when the larva is about to form its chrysalis.

Proboscis: Found on butterflies, it is a coiled feeding tube that adult butterflies use to feed.

Proleg: Any of the false legs on the posterior segment of the caterpillar.

Protandry: Refers to the earlier arrival of males when butterflies emerge from their chrysalis.

Prothorax: The first segment of the thorax.

Pulvillus: The pad that is found between the tarsal claws.

Puddling: When there is a gathering of butterflies at a mud puddle.

Pupa: The hard casing that a caterpillar creates around itself while it is transforming into a butterfly. Also known as a chrysalis.

Pupal Mating: When a adult male butterfly will seek out a female butterfly still in her chrysalis and mate with her as she is emerging.

Pupate: The act of transforming into a chrysalis or pupa.

Radial Veins: The veins in the wings that end in the apical area.

Range: referring to the geographical area that a population of butterflies live in.

Rejection Behavior: This is a behavior that is seen in female butterflies that discourage a male during the mating process.

Relict: A species of butterflies that was left behind in a geographical area after a change in either the climate or landscape.

Reproductive Isolating Barriers: Genetic characteristics and features that prevent butterflies from breeding with other species of butterflies.

Sacculus: A pouch that is located at the base of the valve.

Saccus: A structure in the male reproductive organs.

Scales: Small, modified hairs that cover the wings and body of the butterfly. The color of the butterfly is a result of these hairs.

Scape: The term referring to the base of the antennae.

Sclerite: refers to any hardened plate on the exoskeleton.

Scolus: This refers to the spine on any caterpillar that has a branching spine.

Secondary Seta: The hairs that grow on a caterpillar from the first instar.

Segment: This is used to describe any section on the caterpillar or butterfly that has several sections. This can be appendages, or the abdomen.

Selection Pressure: When the environment, such as lack of food, forces mating patterns in the butterflies, such as a drop in reproduction rate.

Semivoltine: Having one flight every other year.

Seta: Refers to any bristle, spine or hair that protrudes from the exoskeleton.

Sexual Dimorphism: When there are distinct features and characteristics between the male and female of the species.

Sexual Mosaic: A butterfly that has both male and female characteristics.

Sibling Species: Species that are very similar that they are almost unrecognizable as different.

Species: A group of organisms that share the same genes and are isolated from other groups. The monarch butterfly is a species of butterfly.

Speciose: A species that has a large number.

Spermatheca: The organ where sperm is stored in the female butterfly after breeding.

Spermatogenesis: When sperm begins to form. This occurs in the later instars of the larval stage for male butterflies.

Spermatophore: A package that contains sperm and nutrients for egg creation that is deposited to the female by the male butterfly during mating.

Sperm Precedence: A common mechanism in butterflies where a competing male's sperm inactivates any sperm left over in the female from previous matings.

Sphragis: A waxy plug that is inserted into the female reproductive entry in butterflies by the male butterfly. This prevents the female butterfly from mating again. It is not seen in monarch butterflies.

Spinneret: The lobe that is found on the head of the caterpillar. The caterpillar uses the spinneret to dispense silk.

Spiracle: A series of holes and tubes that are found on the sides of the butterfly's or caterpillar's body. These are respiratory openings.

Spur: Refers to the long, spine like projections found on the tibia.

Stabilizing Selection: When natural selection favors average individuals in the population.

Stigma: Refers to a pheromone that is found on the wing of some male butterflies.

Subgenual Organ: An organ on butterflies and caterpillars that can sense vibrations in substrate.

Submarginal: The part of the wing that is between the median and postbasal areas.

Subspecies: A taxon that is similar to a species but with some genetic variations.

Sulcus: An internal ridge that strengthens the exoskeleton.

Suture: Any line on the exoskeleton that is visible.

Sympatric: When something occurs in the same area.

Synchornic: When butterflies or insects are active at the same time or in the same season.

Synonymy: A term that refers to the chronological list of scientific names to label an organism.

Tail: A projection from the hind wing that is seen on some butterflies.

Tarsal Claws: A curved appendage that is found on the last tarsal segment.

Tarsus: Tarsi in plural, these are the tip of the legs on the adult butterfly.

Tequla: The dorsal flaps that are found between the mesothorax and the forewing.

Teneral: The name that is given to a newly emerged butterfly. These butterfly is not able to fly yet.

Thorax: The part of the caterpillar and butterflies body where the legs and wings are attached.

Tibia: A term referring to the fourth segment of the leg.

Tibial Tuft: Tufts of hairs that are found on the tibia.

Tornos: The junction that is found at the inner and outer junctions of the forewing and hindwing.

Torpor: A period of inactivity that is usually induced by environmental conditions.

Treetopping: A behavior seen in male butterflies where they will rest on treetops to wait for a female.

Trochanter: The second segment of the leg.

Tubercle: A round projection that is seen on the body of the caterpillar or pupa.

Uncus: A hook-like structure that is found in the male genitalia. It allows the male to connect with the female.

Univoltine: A butterfly species that only has one flight per year.

Valva: The two appendages that hold the female during mating. Also known as a clasper.

Vein: The tubular struts in the butterfly's wing.

Venation: The arrangement of the veins in the wing.

Ventral: The undersurface of the butterfly. It can only be seen when the wings are closed over the body of the butterfly.

Vinculum: A portion of the male genitals.

Voltinism: Referring to the number of flights per year.